WOULD Y

HAVE A COUGH
- *OR* -
HAVE A SORE THROAT?

RUN OUT OF THE ROOM WHEN A
SCARY SCENE IN A MOVIE
CAME ON
- *OR* -
CLOSE YOUR EYES TIGHT
WHEN A SCARY SCENE IN A
MOVIE CAME ON?

WOULD YOU RATHER...

EAT AN ENTIRE CAKE ON YOUR OWN
- OR -
12 BOXES OF PIZZA ON YOUR OWN?

ALL YOUR TEETH FALL OUT
- OR -
TO HAVE ONLY TWO TEETH?

WOULD YOU RATHER...

BE A UNICORN
- OR -
HAVE A UNICORN OF YOUR
OWN?

HAVE SOMETHING STUCK IN
YOUR TEETH AND NOT KNOW
- OR -
SOMETHING DANGLING OUT
OF YOUR NOSE AND NOT KNOW?

WOULD YOU RATHER...

WATCH SOMEONE ELSE DRAW
- OR -
BE ABLE TO DRAW?

ALWAYS BE AN HOUR EARLY TO
EVERYWHERE YOU GO
- OR -
ALWAYS BE AN HOUR LATE TO
EVERYWHERE YOU GO?

WOULD YOU RATHER...

SING WITH A CROOKED VOICE
IN FRONT OF YOUR
SCHOOLMATES
- OR -
IN FRONT OF COMPLETE
STRANGERS?

NEVER GET TO SEE YOUR
CRUSH AGAIN
- OR -
HAVE THE ENTIRE SCHOOL
KNOW WHO YOU'RE CRUSHING
ON?

WOULD YOU RATHER...

GO SEE A REAL LIFE SHIP
- OR -
GET A TOY BOAT?

HAVE A ROBOT THAT CAN DO
ANYTHING YOU ASK
- OR -
HAVE A ROBOT FRIEND?

WOULD YOU RATHER...

BE THE 1ST FASTEST SWIMMER
IN THE WORLD
- OR -
THE 2ND FASTEST RUNNER IN
THE WORLD?

GET PRESENTS YOU DON'T
LIKE ON YOUR BIRTHDAY
- OR -
GET NO PRESENTS AT ALL?

WOULD YOU RATHER...

BE ABLE TO MAKE YOUR WORST
FOOD DISAPPEAR INTO THIN
AIR
- OR -
BE ABLE TO MAKE YOUR
FAVORITE FOOD APPEAR OUT
OF THIN AIR?

RIDE IN YOUR OWN
HELICOPTER
- OR -
IN OWN A PERSONAL JET?

WOULD YOU RATHER...

FORGET THE WAY TO SCHOOL
– OR –
FORGET THE WAY TO YOUR CLASS?

SMILE ALL THE TIME
– OR –
FROWN ALL THE TIME?

WOULD YOU RATHER...

RELAX BESIDE THE POOL
- OR -
GO SWIMMING?

RAISE CHICKENS
- OR -
COWS?

WOULD YOU RATHER...

BE ABLE TO READ THE MINDS
OF BABIES
- OR -
ABLE TO COMMUNICATE WITH
BABIES?

EAT OATMEAL
- OR -
CEREAL?

WOULD YOU RATHER...

CUDDLE A BIG TEDDY
- OR -
CUDDLE WITH MOM?

FART IN AN ELEVATOR ON
YOUR WAY TO CLASS
- OR -
FART IN CLASS?

WOULD YOU RATHER...

BE SUPER FAMOUS FOR DOING
SOMETHING BAD
- OR -
DO SOMETHING AMAZING THAT
NO ONE WILL EVER KNOW
ABOUT?

BE ABLE TO MEET YOUR
ANCESTORS
- OR -
YOUR GREAT
GRANDCHILDREN?

WOULD YOU RATHER...

SLEEP ALL DAY
- **OR** -
HAVE TO STAY UP ALL NIGHT?

HAVE THE POWER TO SEE
THROUGH WALLS
- **OR** -
THE ABILITY TO WALK
THROUGH WALLS?

WOULD YOU RATHER...

WAKE UP EARLY
- OR -
GO TO BED EARLY?

DO THE LAUNDRY ALL ON YOUR OWN
- OR -
HELP MOM WITH THE LAUNDRY?

WOULD YOU RATHER...

HAVE A JETPACK
- OR -
HAVE YOUR OWN ROBOT?

HAVE 6 FINGERS
- OR -
6 TOES?

WOULD YOU RATHER...

FIND LOTS OF EASTER EGGS
- OR -
MEET THE EASTER BUNNY?

HAVE 3 ARMS
- OR -
ONLY 1 LEG?

WOULD YOU RATHER...

GO WITH MOM TO WORK
- OR -
HAVE YOUR MOM STAY AT
HOME ALL DAY?

HAVE CLAWS AS HANDS
- OR -
A HOOK AS A HAND?

WOULD YOU RATHER...

EAT FISH THAT'S HALF BURNT
– OR –
EAT FISH THAT'S HALF DONE?

BE ABLE TO PLAY ANY
MUSICAL INSTRUMENT THAT
THERE IS
– OR –
BE ABLE TO SPEAK EVERY
LANGUAGE THERE IS?

WOULD YOU RATHER...

LOSE YOUR FAVORITE TEDDY
BEAR
- OR -
LOSE YOUR FAVORITE
BLANKET?

HAVE HAIR GROW ON YOUR
TONGUE
- OR -
HAVE HAIR GROW IN BETWEEN
YOUR TEETH?

WOULD YOU RATHER...

NEVER GET TO EAT DONUTS
FOR THE REST OF YOUR LIFE
- OR -
EAT ONLY DONUTS FOR AN
ENTIRE WEEK?

HAVE A PICTURE OF YOUR
FAVORITE HERO
- OR -
HAVE A WALL POSTER OF YOUR
FAVORITE HERO?

WOULD YOU RATHER...

HAVE POOP THAT SMELLS LIKE
STRAWBERRY
- OR -
POOP CHOCOLATE?

LIVE ON A HOUSEBOAT
- OR -
LIVE IN A TREE HOUSE?

WOULD YOU RATHER...

HAVE TO SHOUT AT FULL VOLUME WHENEVER YOU SPOKE
- OR -
BE UNABLE TO TALK EVER AGAIN?

BE STUCK IN A TOILET BECAUSE THE TOILET DOOR WON'T OPEN
- OR -
BECAUSE YOUR POOP WON'T FLUSH?

WOULD YOU RATHER...

BE SURROUNDED BY ANNOYING
PEOPLE
- *OR* -
HAVE NO FRIENDS?

DRINK ORANGE JUICE
- *OR* -
SUCK ON AN ORANGE?

WOULD YOU RATHER...

GET A FREE PLANE TICKET
- OR -
GET A FREE BOAT CRUISE?

FORGET YOU HAVE FEARS
- OR -
FACE YOUR FEARS?

WOULD YOU RATHER...

HAVE JUST ONE SUPERPOWER
FOR A MONTH
- OR -
HAVE A LOT OF SUPERPOWERS
FOR ONE WEEK?

WIN A CASH PRIZE
- OR -
A MYSTERY ITEM?

WOULD YOU RATHER...

LOOK REALLY OLD
- OR -
LOOK LIKE A NEWBORN BABY
AGAIN?

EAT SOMETHING ROASTED
- OR -
SOMETHING FRIED?

WOULD YOU RATHER...

SWIM IN ICE-COLD WATER
- OR -
IN A POOL OF HOT WATER?

HAVE AN AUNT THAT PATS
YOUR HEAD A LOT
- OR -
HAVE AN AUNT THAT PULLS
YOUR CHEEKS A LOT?

WOULD YOU RATHER...

HAVE A CHICKEN LAY EGGS IN YOUR HAIR
- OR -
HAVE A BIRD MAKE A NEST IN YOUR HAIR?

HAVE THE ABILITY TO BECOME INVISIBLE
- OR -
HAVE THE POWER TO READ PEOPLE'S MINDS?

WOULD YOU RATHER...

THROW UP ON YOUR CRUSH
- OR -
THROW UP ON YOUR BEST
FRIEND?

HAVE REALLY LONG HAIR
- OR -
BE BALD?

WOULD YOU RATHER...

HAVE ALL THE JUNK FOOD YOU
COULD EVER WANT
- OR -
HAVE ALL THE DRINKS YOU
COULD EVER WANT?

GET ASSIGNMENTS EVERY
SINGLE DAY FOR A YEAR
- OR -
BE STUCK IN SCHOOL FOR A
YEAR?

WOULD YOU RATHER...

BRUSH YOUR TEETH WITH
KETCHUP
- OR -
WITH HOT SAUCE?

GET LOTS OF CUDDLES
- OR -
GET LOTS OF HUGS?

WOULD YOU RATHER...

SHARE YOUR BED WITH
SOMEONE WHO FARTS A LOT
- OR -
SHARE YOUR BED WITH
SOMEONE WHO PEES ON THE
BED?

PLAY INSIDE
- OR -
OUTSIDE?

WOULD YOU RATHER...

KNOW HOW TO READ LIPS
- OR -
KNOW AND UNDERSTAND SIGN
LANGUAGE?

KNOW HOW TO SPEAK SPANISH
FLUENTLY
- OR -
KNOW HOW TO SPEAK FRENCH
FLUENTLY?

WOULD YOU RATHER...

GO TO A DANCE WITH
SOMEONE WHO HAS BODY ODOR
- OR -
GO TO A DANCE WITH
SOMEONE WHO HAS BAD BREATH?

BRUSH YOUR TEETH USING A
BAR OF SOAP
- OR -
USING TWO-MONTH-OLD MILK?

WOULD YOU RATHER...

FORGET TO TAKE YOUR
TOOTHBRUSH FOR A SLEEPOVER
- OR -
FORGET TO TAKE YOUR
TOWEL FOR A SLEEPOVER?

HAVE NOISY FRIENDS
- OR -
HAVE NOSY FRIENDS?

WOULD YOU RATHER...

BE PRANKED
- OR -
BE A WELL-KNOWN PRANKSTER?

BE POPULAR AMONG YOUR
CLASSMATES
- OR -
BE POPULAR AMONG YOUR
TEACHERS?

WOULD YOU RATHER...

TO NEVER BE ABLE TO LISTEN
TO MUSIC AGAIN
- OR -
ONLY BE ABLE TO LISTEN TO
MUSIC FROM THE 60'S?

TO UNDERSTAND WHAT YOU
READ REALLY FAST
- OR -
BE ABLE TO READ REALLY
FAST?

WOULD YOU RATHER...

OWN 10 PUPPIES
- OR -
10 KITTENS?

DRIVE IN A CAR
- OR -
FLY IN A PLANE?

WOULD YOU RATHER...

HAVE A NANNY THAT'S BORING
- OR -
HAVE A NANNY THAT MAKES
TERRIBLE MEALS?

BE ABLE TO DRAW AMAZINGLY
WELL
- OR -
ABLE TO SING REALLY,
REALLY WELL?

WOULD YOU RATHER...

LIVE IN THE SKY
PERMANENTLY
- OR -
UNDERWATER PERMANENTLY?

HAVE EYES THAT CHANGE
COLOR DEPENDING ON THE
MOOD THAT YOU'RE IN
- OR -
HAVE HAIR THAT CHANGES
COLOR BASED ON THE
TEMPERATURE?

WOULD YOU RATHER...

SWIM OUTDOORS
- *OR* -
SWIM INDOORS?

GET COTTON CANDY
- *OR* -
ICE-CREAM AT A PARK?

WOULD YOU RATHER...

LEAVE YOUR MONEY WITH MOM
- OR -
LEAVE YOUR MONEY WITH DAD?

HAVE A CAR THAT CAN DRIVE UNDERWATER
- OR -
HAVE A FLYING CARPET?

WOULD YOU RATHER...

HAVE MILK RUN DOWN YOUR
NOSE EVERY TIME YOU LAUGH
– OR –
HAVE MILK RUN OUT OF YOUR
EYES EVERY TIME YOU
CRIED?

BE THE WORLD'S RICHEST
PERSON
– OR –
HAVE THREE FREE WISHES?

WOULD YOU RATHER...

HAVE MUD SPLASHED ALL OVER
YOU
- OR -
ROLL IN MUD?

HAVE REALLY WHITE SKIN
- OR -
HAVE BLUE SKIN LIKE AN
ALIEN?

WOULD YOU RATHER...

LIVE IN A REALLY NOISY
NEIGHBORHOOD
- OR -
IN A REALLY QUIET
NEIGHBORHOOD?

MEET A MONSTER WHO'S
LOOKING FOR FOOD
- OR -
MEET A FRIENDLY MONSTER?

WOULD YOU RATHER...

DRINK CHOCOLATE MILK
- OR -
DRINK HOT CHOCOLATE?

HAVE YOUR LEG STUCK IN THE
TOILET BOWL
- OR -
YOUR HANDS STUCK IN THE
TOILET BOWL?

WOULD YOU RATHER...

HAVE MILKSHAKES
- OR -
A SMOOTHIE?

GO OUTSIDE AND PLAY WITH
YOUR FRIENDS
- OR -
HAVE YOUR FRIENDS COME
OVER?

WOULD YOU RATHER...

HAVE A LIBRARY IN YOUR
HOUSE
- OR -
GO TO THE LIBRARY?

EAT HOMEMADE FOOD
- OR -
EAT FAST FOOD?

WOULD YOU RATHER...

HAVE HAIR THAT'S ALMOST
TOUCHING THE FLOOR
- OR -
BE BALD?

PEE WITH YOUR MOUTH
- OR -
DRINK WITH YOUR NOSE?

WOULD YOU RATHER...

LICK YOUR FOOT
- OR -
YOUR FRIEND'S FOOT?

NEVER BE ABLE TO SMELL
AGAIN
- OR -
BE ABLE TO SMELL ONLY BAD-
SMELLING THINGS?

WOULD YOU RATHER...

BE THE BRIGHTEST KID IN
YOUR WHOLE SCHOOL
- *OR* -
BE THE BEST AT SPORTS IN
YOUR SCHOOL?

READ A HARDCOVER BOOK
- *OR* -
LISTEN TO AN AUDIOBOOK?

WOULD YOU RATHER...

GO TO A CLOTHING STORE
- OR -
TO A TOY STORE?

STICK YOUR FACE INTO A
PLATE OF BLENDED GARLIC
- OR -
INTO A PLATE OF VINEGAR?

WOULD YOU RATHER...

HAVE LARGE HANDS
- OR -
HAVE LARGE FEET?

HAVE TISSUE PAPER STUCK TO
THE BOTTOM OF YOUR SHOE
- OR -
HAVE GUM STUCK TO THE
BOTTOM OF YOUR SHOE?

WOULD YOU RATHER...

HAVE A BABYSITTER WHO'S
REALLY YOUNG
- OR -
HAVE A BABYSITTER WHO'S
REALLY OLD?

HAVE THE POWER TO
COMMUNICATE WITH ANIMALS
- OR -
BE ABLE TO CHANGE INTO AN
ANIMAL OF YOUR CHOICE?

WOULD YOU RATHER...

MEET AN ALIEN
- OR -
MEET GOD?

BRUSH A HORSE
- OR -
FEED A HORSE?

WOULD YOU RATHER...

WEAR DORA THE EXPLORER
PAJAMAS
- OR -
WEAR SPONGEBOB PAJAMAS?

THE TOOTH FAIRY LEFT A
GOLDEN TOOTH
- OR -
THE TOOTH FAIRY RAN OFF
WITH YOUR TOOTH AND LEFT
NOTHING?

WOULD YOU RATHER...

NEVER HAVE CANDY, EVER
AGAIN
- OR -
TO ONLY EAT CANDY FOR THE
REST OF YOUR LIFE?

SNEAK INTO YOUR NEIGHBOR'S
HOUSE WHILE THEY'RE ASLEEP
- OR -
SPY ON YOUR NEIGHBOR?

WOULD YOU RATHER...

WAKE UP WITH WINGS
- OR -
WAKE UP WITH A TAIL?

SEE A SHOOTING STAR
- OR -
A RAINBOW?

WOULD YOU RATHER...

BE ABLE TO SPIT OUT FIRE
- OR -
BE ABLE TO SPIT OUT ICE?

NOT HAVE TOILET PAPER
WHILE YOU'RE ON THE TOILET
SEAT
- OR -
HAVE WATER TO WASH YOUR
HANDS WITH AFTERWARD?

WOULD YOU RATHER...

BE REALLY GOOD AT A SPORT
- OR -
GET GOOD GRADES?

LIVE IN A CAVE ALONE
- OR -
IN A CAVE WITH A FRIENDLY
BEAR?

WOULD YOU RATHER...

HAVE A PET DINOSAUR
- OR -
HAVE A PET DRAGON?

BE ON A TINY BOAT
- OR -
ON A GIANT SHIP?

WOULD YOU RATHER...

SOMEONE WHO TALKS IN THEIR SLEEP
- OR -
SHARE YOUR BED WITH SOMEONE WHO SNORES?

GIVE YOUR ALREADY CHEWED GUM TO SOMEONE ELSE
- OR -
EAT A PIECE OF GUM FROM THE STREET?

WOULD YOU RATHER...

GO SKYDIVING
- OR -
GO BUNGEE JUMPING?

MEET A CLOWN
- OR -
BE A CLOWN?

WOULD YOU RATHER...

HAVE THE ABILITY TO TALK
TO ANIMALS
- OR -
BE ABLE TO HEAR ANIMALS
TALK?

BE PART OF A SET OF TWINS
- OR -
BE PART OF A SET OF
TRIPLETS?

WOULD YOU RATHER...

RIDE THE BENCH ON A SPORTS TEAM THAT ALWAYS WINS
- OR -
BE THE STAR PLAYER ON A LOSING SPORTS TEAM AT SCHOOL?

BE PRANKED WITH A FAKE BUG
- OR -
BE PRANKED WITH A FAKE RAT?

WOULD YOU RATHER...

LOOK LIKE AN OLD PERSON
- OR -
SOUND LIKE AN OLD PERSON?

MOVE TO ANOTHER COUNTRY
- OR -
LIVE WHERE YOU ARE
FOREVER?

WOULD YOU RATHER...

HAVE HAIR THAT TASTES LIKE CANDY
- OR -
HAVE MULTICOLORED HAIR?

WEAR UNCLEAN CLOTHES FOR A WEEK
- OR -
WEAR THE SAME OUTFIT EVERY DAY FOR A WEEK?

WOULD YOU RATHER...

GO CAMPING
- OR -
GO FISHING?

GET A CAVITY FILLED BY
YOUR DENTIST
- OR -
RECEIVE A SHOT FROM YOUR
DOCTOR?

WOULD YOU RATHER...

HELP WITH THE COOKING
- OR -
PUT UP CHRISTMAS
DECORATIONS?

HAVE A WATER BALLOON
FIGHT
- OR -
A SNOWBALL FIGHT?

WOULD YOU RATHER...

BE A PART OF A CIRCUS SHOW
- OR -
GO WATCH A CIRCUS SHOW?

SING EVERY TIME YOU HEARD
A SONG
- OR -
HAVE TO DANCE EVERY TIME
YOU HEARD A SONG?

WOULD YOU RATHER...

NEVER EAT FAST FOOD AGAIN
- OR -
EAT FAST FOOD FOR EVERY
SINGLE MEAL FOR THE REST
OF YOUR LIFE?

HAVE REALLY LONG TOENAILS
- OR -
HAVE REALLY LONG
FINGERNAILS?

WOULD YOU RATHER...

PEE IN YOUR PANTS WHILE WATCHING A SCARY MOVIE
- OR -
SCREAM WHILE WATCHING A SCARY MOVIE?

TRAVEL ANYWHERE IN THE WORLD
- OR -
TRAVEL TO ANY POINT THROUGH TIME?

WOULD YOU RATHER...

BE GIVEN APPLES TO EAT
- OR -
GIVEN VEGETABLES TO EAT?

BE REALLY HUGE
- OR -
REALLY STRONG?

WOULD YOU RATHER...

BE IN A DANCE CLASS
- OR -
IN THE CHOIR?

HAVE 3 CATS
- OR -
1 DOG?

WOULD YOU RATHER...

EAT SOMETHING REALLY HOT
- OR -
SOMETHING REALLY COLD?

WAKE UP SUPER EARLY
- OR -
STAY UP REALLY LATE?

WOULD YOU RATHER...

HAVE A REALLY SCARY SMILE
- OR -
A REALLY LOUD LAUGH?

BE WITHOUT A NOSE
- OR -
WITHOUT EARS?

WOULD YOU RATHER...

BESIDE SOMEONE YOU'VE
NEVER SEEN BEFORE
- *OR* -
WAKE UP BESIDE A CARTOON
CHARACTER?

BE ABLE TO SPEAK FIVE
DIFFERENT LANGUAGES
- *OR* -
KNOW THE LYRICS TO EVERY
SONG EVER WRITTEN?

WOULD YOU RATHER...

PLAY ON THE TRAMPOLINE
- OR -
PLAY ON THE SLIDES?

DANCE AROUND YOUR HOUSE IN
YOUR UNDERWEAR
- OR -
DANCE AROUND THE
NEIGHBORHOOD BAREFOOTED?

WOULD YOU RATHER...

FINID A COCKROACH HIDING IN YOUR SHOE
- OR -
FIND A COCKROACH HIDING IN YOUR PIZZA?

THAT IT WAS CHRISTMAS EVERY DAY
- OR -
THAT IT WAS YOUR BIRTHDAY EVERY DAY?

WOULD YOU RATHER...

LIVE IN A WORLD FULL OF
ALIENS
- OR -
LIVE IN A WORLD FULL OF
ZOMBIES?

HAVE SODA COME BACK OUT OF
YOUR MOUTH
- OR -
HAVE SODA COME OUT OF YOUR
NOSE?

WOULD YOU RATHER...

OWN A MOUSE-SIZED ELEPHANT
- OR -
OWN AN ELEPHANT-SIZED
MOUSE?

FEEL TOO COLD
- OR -
TOO HOT?

WOULD YOU RATHER...

TRAVEL BACK TO THE PAST
- OR -
INTO THE FUTURE?

HAVE PIZZA
- OR -
A HOTDOG?

WOULD YOU RATHER...

NEVER HAVE TO DO HOMEWORK
AGAIN
- OR -
NEVER TAKE A TEST AGAIN?

BE A TEACHER
- OR -
BE A DOCTOR?

WOULD YOU RATHER...

EAT SOMETHING THAT'S
PEPPERY
- OR -
SOMETHING THAT'S SPICY?

BE UNABLE TO EVER LEAVE
THE STATE YOU LIVE IN
AGAIN
- OR -
TAKE A TRIP AROUND THE
WORLD BUT NEVER BE ABLE TO
STOP TO SEE ANYTHING?

WOULD YOU RATHER...

HAVE YOUR BEST FRIEND WEAR
A CLOWN'S COSTUME
- OR -
WEAR A CLOWN'S COSTUME
YOURSELF?

HIDE INSIDE YOUR CLOSET
- OR -
HIDE UNDER YOUR BED?

WOULD YOU RATHER...

TOUCH DOG POOP
- OR -
TOUCH YOUR POOP?

LIVE IN A HOUSE WITH NO
RUNNING WATER
- OR -
LIVE IN A HOUSE WITH NO
POWER?

WOULD YOU RATHER...

HAVE ANY FOOD YOU EVER
WANTED
- OR -
TO HAVE ALL THE TOYS YOU
EVER WANTED?

HAVE A BIG BACKYARD
- OR -
HAVE A BIG ROOM?

WOULD YOU RATHER...

EAT A WHOLE CAKE TO YOURSELF
- OR -
A BIG BOWL OF ICE CREAM?

THAT IT WAS SUMMER ALL THE TIME
- OR -
IT WAS WINTER ALL THE TIME?

WOULD YOU RATHER...

HOP DOWN THE STAIRS
- OR -
ROLL DOWN THE STAIRS?

GET FIVE CONCERT TICKETS
FOR FREE
- OR -
MEET YOUR FAVORITE BAND?

WOULD YOU RATHER...

GET BRAND NEW SOCKS
- OR -
FIND YOUR FAVORITE SOCKS
THAT WENT MISSING?

HAVE NO TONGUE
- OR -
HAVE TWO TONGUES?

WOULD YOU RATHER...

BE PAID TO DO YOUR
HOMEWORK
- *OR* -
NEVER HAVE HOMEWORK
AGAIN?

GO TO A REGULAR SCHOOL
- *OR* -
BE HOMESCHOOLED?

WOULD YOU RATHER...

STAR IN A MOVIE
- OR -
BE THE AUTHOR OF A BEST-
SELLING A BOOK?

GET INTO A FIGHT WITH
DUCKS
- OR -
CHASED BY DUCKS?

WOULD YOU RATHER...

BE SHIPWREAKED ALONE ON A
DESERT ISLAND
- OR -
STUCK THERE WITH SOMEONE
WHO WON'T STOP SCREAMING?

PEE ON YOURSELF WHEN
SCARED
- OR -
POOP IN YOUR PANTS WHEN
SCARED?

WOULD YOU RATHER...

HAVE THE POWER TO FLY
- OR -
THE ABILITY TO BREATHE
UNDERWATER?

BE THIRSTY ALLT HE TIME,
- OR -
BE HUNGRY ALL THE TIME?

WOULD YOU RATHER...

FORGET YOUR LINES DURING
A DEBATE IN FRONT OF THE
ENTIRE SCHOOL
- OR -
FORGET YOUR LINES DURING
A CLASS PRESENTATION?

BE A FISH
- OR -
BE A BIRD?

WOULD YOU RATHER...

EAT YOUR CHIPS WITH
KETCHUP
- OR -
YOUR CHIPS WITH MUSTARD?

EAT BREAD WITH JAM
- OR -
EAT BREAD WITH BUTTER?

WOULD YOU RATHER...

TICKLE YOUR DAD WHILE HE'S
SLEEPING
- OR -
YOUR MOM SHE SLEEPING?

GET A TREAT
- OR -
GET A TRICK?

WOULD YOU RATHER...

PEE IN A POOL
- *OR* -
SWIM IN A POOL THAT YOUR
BEST FRIEND PEED IN?

HAVE A RABBIT'S TEETH
- *OR* -
A RABBIT'S EARS?

WOULD YOU RATHER...

MEET SOMEONE WITH TWO
MOUTHS
– OR –
MEET SOMEONE WHO HAS THREE
EYES?

WEAR SHOES THAT ARE MUCH
BIGGER THAN YOUR FEET
– OR –
WEAR UGLY SHOES?

WOULD YOU RATHER...

MOVE TO ANOTHER COUNTRY
- OR -
LIVE WHERE YOU ARE
FOREVER?

GO TO SCHOOL IN THE CAR
WITH YOUR MOM AND DAD
- OR -
GO TO SCHOOL WITH YOUR
FRIEND ON THE PUBLIC BUS?

WOULD YOU RATHER...

BLOW A BALLOON TILL IT
POPS
- OR -
POP A BALLOON WITH
SOMETHING SHARP?

BE IN A DANCE CLASS
- OR -
BE IN THE CHOIR?

WOULD YOU RATHER...

HAVE NOISY FRIENDS
- OR -
HAVE NOSEY FRIENDS?

HAVE ONLY MULTICOLORED
CLOTHES
- OR -
HAVE ONLY WHITE CLOTHES?

WOULD YOU RATHER...

LIVE WITH GRANDMA
- OR -
LIVE WITH YOUR COUSINS?

DRINK CHOCOLATE MILK
- OR -
DRINK HOT CHOCOLATE?

WOULD YOU RATHER...

GET ASSIGNMENTS EVERY SINGLE DAY FOR A YEAR
- *OR* -
BE STUCK IN SCHOOL FOR A YEAR?

HAVE NO NOSE AT ALL
- *OR* -
HAVE A NOSE AS LONG AS PINOCCHIO'S?

WOULD YOU RATHER...

STAIN YOUR MOUTH WITH
CHICKEN SAUCE AND NOT
KNOW
- OR -
STAIN YOUR HANDS WITH
CHICKEN SAUCE AND NOT
HAVE ANYTHING TO CLEAN
IT WITH?

LOSE ALL YOUR BABY
PICTURES
- OR -
LOSE ALL THE PICTURES
FROM YOUR LAST BIRTHDAY?

WOULD YOU RATHER...

HAVE A BABY PEE ON YOU
- OR -
HAVE A BABY THROW UP ON
YOU?

HAVE REALLY LONG
TOENAILS
- OR -
HAVE REALLY LONG
FINGERNAILS?

WOULD YOU RATHER...

HAVE A CHICKEN LAY EGGS
IN YOUR HAIR
- *OR* -
HAVE A BIRD MAKE A NEST
IN YOUR HAIR?

TRAVEL BY AIRPLANE
- *OR* -
TRAVEL BY HOT AIR
BALLOON?

WOULD YOU RATHER...

LIVE ON A HOUSEBOAT
- OR -
LIVE IN A TREE HOUSE?

BE PRANKED
- OR -
BE A WELL-KNOWN
PRANKSTER?

WOULD YOU RATHER...

HAVE TO POOP EVERY HOUR
- OR -
HAVE TO PEE EVERY HOUR?

HAVE YOUR OWN A JETPACK
- OR -
HAVE YOUR OWN ROBOT?

WOULD YOU RATHER...

RIDE THE BENCH ON A
SPORTS TEAM THAT ALWAYS
WINS
- OR -
BE THE STAR PLAYER ON A
LOSING SPORTS TEAM AT
SCHOOL?

GIVE YOUR ALREADY
CHEWED GUM TO SOMEONE
ELSE
- OR -
EAT A PIECE OF GUM FROM
THE STREET?

WOULD YOU RATHER...

BE STUCK WITH A CLOWN
THAT'S QUITE ANNOYING
- OR -
BE STUCK IN A ROOM WITH A
CLOWN THAT'S NOT FUNNY?

A MAGIC WIZARD
- OR -
BE A SUPERHERO?

WOULD YOU RATHER...

HAVE THE POWER TO
TRANSFORM INTO A
BUTTERFLY
- OR -
TO TRANSFORM INTO AN
EAGLE?

GET COTTON CANDY
- OR -
ICE-CREAM AT A PARK?

WOULD YOU RATHER...

MEET A CLOWN
- OR -
BE A CLOWN?

HAVE BADLY TRIMMED HAIR
- OR -
HAVE SMELLY HAIR?

WOULD YOU RATHER...

EAT FISH THAT'S HALF BURNT
- OR -
EAT FISH THAT'S HALF DONE?

HAVE CLAWS AS HANDS
- OR -
HOOKS AS A HAND?

WOULD YOU RATHER...

HAVE THE BUTTON ON YOUR
JEANS FALL OFF
- *OR* -
HAVE THE ZIP OF YOUR
JEANS CUT?

TAKE A DAY TRIP TO THE
BEACH
- *OR* -
TAKE A DAY TRIP TO THE
ZOO?

WOULD YOU RATHER...

BE THE 1ST FASTEST
SWIMMER IN THE WORLD
- OR -
THE 2ND FASTEST RUNNER IN
THE WORLD?

BE SUPERMAN'S SIDEKICK
- OR -
BE SPIDERMAN'S SIDEKICK?

WOULD YOU RATHER...

HAVE A HUNDRED MILLION
DOLLARS WORTH OF CANDY
- OR -
HAVE A MILLION DOLLARS IN
PENNIES?

HAVE MILK RUN DOWN YOUR
NOSE EVERY TIME YOU
LAUGH
- OR -
HAVE MILK RUN OUT OF
YOUR EYES EVERY TIME
YOU CRIED?

WOULD YOU RATHER...

YOUR HANDS GOT DIRTY ALL THE TIME
- OR -
YOUR FEET GOT DIRTY ALL THE TIME?

RIDE ON A LION
- OR -
RIDE ON THE BACK OF A TIGER?

WOULD YOU RATHER...

WAKE UP WITH WINGS
- *OR* -
WAKE UP WITH A TAIL?

WEAR TRENDY SNEAKERS
- *OR* -
WEAR CUTE SHOES?

WOULD YOU RATHER...

BE A PART OF A CIRCUS
SHOW
- OR -
GO WATCH A CIRCUS SHOW?

LIVE IN A CAVE ALONE
- OR -
LIVE IN A CAVE WITH A
FRIENDLY BEAR?

WOULD YOU RATHER...

HAVE A HOLE IN YOUR
OUTFIT AND NOT NOTICE
- OR -
HAVE A STAIN ON YOUR
OUTFIT AND NOT NOTICE?

MAKE BURPS THAT SMELL
REALLY BAD
- OR -
MAKE LOUD BURPS THAT ARE
HARD TO IGNORE?

WOULD YOU RATHER...

GO OUTSIDE AND PLAY WITH YOUR FRIENDS
- OR -
HAVE YOUR FRIENDS COME OVER?

MEET A FAIRY
- OR -
A GODDESS?

WOULD YOU RATHER...

WEAR DORA THE EXPLORER PAJAMAS
- OR -
WEAR SPONGEBOB PAJAMAS?

SHARE YOUR BED WITH SOMEONE WHO FARTS A LOT
- OR -
SHARE YOUR BED WITH SOMEONE WHO PEES ON THE BED?

WOULD YOU RATHER...

PLAY GAMES ON A PHONE
- *OR* -
PLAY A BOARD GAME?

BE THE HEAD OF THE FBI
FOR THE PRESIDENT
- *OR* -
BE A SUPERHERO THAT
NEVER GAINS
RECOGNITION?

WOULD YOU RATHER...

BE AN INTERNET SENSATION
FROM DOING SOMETHING
NERDY
- OR -
BE AN INTERNET SENSATION
FROM DOING SOMETHING
EMBARRASSING?

BRUSH YOUR TEETH USING A
BAR OF SOAP
- OR -
BRUSH YOUR TEETH USING
TWO-MONTH-OLD MILK?

WOULD YOU RATHER...

NOT HAVE TOILET PAPER
WHILE YOU'RE ON THE
TOILET SEAT
- *OR* -
NOT HAVE WATER TO WASH
YOUR HANDS WITH
AFTERWARD?

BE EATEN BY YOUR DOG
- *OR* -
HAVE YOUR DIARY READ OUT
IN PUBLIC?

WOULD YOU RATHER...

FOLD ALL THE CLOTHES
- OR -
WASH ALL THE DIRTY
CLOTHES?

HAVE A SMALL ZIT THAT
WON'T GO AWAY
- OR -
HAVE A MASSIVE ZIT THAT
WILL POP?

WOULD YOU RATHER...

SLEEP BESIDE A SKUNK
- **OR** -
SLEEP BESIDE A PIG?

BE IN THE DEBATE CLUB
- **OR** -
WATCH A DEBATE?

WOULD YOU RATHER...

BE IN YOUR FAVORITE
VIDEO GAME
- *OR* -
BE IN YOUR FAVORITE
CARTOON?

GO TO A DANCE WITH
SOMEONE WHO HAS BODY ODOR
- *OR* -
GO TO A DANCE WITH
SOMEONE WHO HAS BAD
BREATH?

WOULD YOU RATHER...

MEET A DONKEY THAT TALKS
- *OR* -
MEET A DONKEY THAT WALKS
ON TWO LEGS?

BE A BRAIN SURGEON
- *OR* -
BE A SCIENTIST?

WOULD YOU RATHER...

HAVE THE ABILITY TO TALK
TO ANIMALS
- OR -
BE ABLE TO HEAR ANIMALS
TALK?

NEVER GET TO EAT DONUTS
FOR THE REST OF YOUR LIFE
- OR -
EAT ONLY DONUTS FOR AN
ENTIRE WEEK?

WOULD YOU RATHER...

BE MUCH SHORTER
- OR -
BE MUCH TALLER?

DROP YOUR NEW PHONE DOWN
TO THE TOILET
- OR -
DROP YOUR CHARM
BRACELET DOWN THE SINK?

WOULD YOU RATHER...

HAVE YOUR LEG STUCK IN
THE TOILET BOWL
- OR -
HAVE YOUR HANDS STUCK IN
THE TOILET BOWL?

SEE A FUNNY VIDEO OF
YOUR PARENTS ONLINE
- OR -
SEE A FUNNY VIDEO OF A
CLOSE FRIEND ONLINE?

WOULD YOU RATHER...

BE VERY UNPOPULAR
- OR -
BE SUPER POPULAR AND BE
STALKED BY PAPARAZZI ALL
THE TIME?

LOSE YOUR FAVORITE TOY
- OR -
LOSE ALL YOUR SAVINGS?

WOULD YOU RATHER...

EAT 1 SPIDER
- OR -
A WHOLE BOWL OF WORMS?

WATCH TV IN BED ALONE
- OR -
WATCH TV ON THE COUCH
WITH YOUR FAMILY?

WOULD YOU RATHER...

HAVE TWO REALLY SHORT
LEGS
- OR -
HAVE ONE LEG SHORTER
THAN THE OTHER?

BE ABLE TO DRAW
AMAZINGLY WELL
- OR -
BE ABLE TO SING REALLY,
REALLY WELL?

WOULD YOU RATHER...

A GO TO COSTUME PARTY
- OR -
TO A TEA PARTY?

HAVE AN AUNT THAT PATS
YOUR HEAD A LOT
- OR -
HAVE AN AUNT THAT PULLS
YOUR CHEEKS A LOT?

WOULD YOU RATHER...

BE BITTEN BY A MOSQUITO
10 TIMES
- OR -
BE STUNG BY A BEE 1 TIME?

THROW UP ON YOUR CRUSH
- OR -
THROW UP ON YOUR BEST
FRIEND?

WOULD YOU RATHER...

LOOK LIKE AN OLD PERSON
- *OR* -
SOUND LIKE AN OLD PERSON?

SWIM IN ICE-COLD WATER
- *OR* -
SWIM IN A POOL OF HOT WATER?

WOULD YOU RATHER...

GET A FREE PLANE TICKET
- OR -
GET A FREE BOAT CRUISE?

BE ABLE RUN ON WATER
- OR -
BE ABLE TO BREATHE
UNDERWATER?

WOULD YOU RATHER...

NEVER EAT FAST FOOD
AGAIN
- OR -
EAT FAST FOOD FOR EVERY
SINGLE MEAL FOR THE REST
OF YOUR LIFE?

BE PRANKED WITHH A FAKE
BUG
- OR -
BE PRANKED WITH A FAKE
RAT?

WOULD YOU RATHER...

STOP DRINKING ANYTHING
COLD ALTOGETHER
- OR -
GET A BRAIN FREEZE
EVERY TIME YOU DRANK
SOMETHING COLD?

SEND A PRANK TEXT
- OR -
DO A PRANK PHONE CALL?

WOULD YOU RATHER...

SHOWER WITH HOT WATER
- OR -
SHOWER WITH COLD WATER?

BE UNABLE TO CELEBRATE
HALLOWEEN
- OR -
BE UNABLE TO CELEBRATE
CHRISTMAS?

WOULD YOU RATHER...

FIND LOTS OF EASTER EGGS
- OR -
MEET THE EASTER BUNNY?

HAVE TO SING EVERY TIME
YOU HEARD A SONG
- OR -
HAVE TO DANCE EVERY TIME
YOU HEARD A SONG?

WOULD YOU RATHER...

BE IN A HOUSE FILLED WITH CANDY
- *OR* -
BE IN A HOUSE FILLED WITH MARSHMALLOWS?

GO SKYDIVING
- *OR* -
GO BUNGEE JUMPING?

WOULD YOU RATHER...

HAVE SUPER STRENGTH
- OR -
HAVE SUPER SPEED?

LIVE IN THE SKY
PERMANENTLY
- OR -
UNDERWATER PERMANENTLY?

WOULD YOU RATHER...

NEVER HAVE CANDY, EVER
AGAIN
- OR -
TO ONLY EAT CANDY FOR
THE REST OF YOUR LIFE?

BE STUCK IN A TOILET
BECAUSE THE TOILET DOOR
WON'T OPEN
- OR -
BE STUCK IN A TOILET
BECAUSE YOUR POOP WON'T
FLUSH?

WOULD YOU RATHER...

GO WITH MOM TO WORK
- OR -
HAVE YOUR MOM STAY AT
HOME ALL DAY?

BECOME THE SIZE OF A
WHALE
- OR -
BE SHRUNK DOWN TO THE
SIZE OF A BUG?

WOULD YOU RATHER...

WEAR ANY CLOTHING OF
YOUR CHOICE TO SCHOOL
- OR -
WEAR YOUR SCHOOL UNIFORM
ALL THE TIME?

TELEPORT TO THE SURFACE
OF THE MOON
- OR -
TO THE BOTTOM OF THE
OCEAN?

WOULD YOU RATHER...

EAT ONION-FLAVORED ICE CREAM
- *OR* -
EAT CHICKEN-FLAVORED COOKIES?

PLAY INSIDE
- *OR* -
PLAY OUTSIDE?

WOULD YOU RATHER...

DRESS UP AS CARTOON
CHARACTERS
- OR -
WATCH CARTOONS?

BE ABLE TO PLAY ANY
MUSICAL INSTRUMENT THAT
THERE IS
- OR -
BE ABLE TO SPEAK EVERY
LANGUAGE THERE IS?

WOULD YOU RATHER...

HAVE 3 ARMS
- OR -
ONLY 1 LEG?

BE PART OF A SET OF TWINS
- OR -
PART OF A SET OF
TRIPLETS?

WOULD YOU RATHER...

BE ABLE TO SEW
- OR -
BE ABLE TO KNIT?

TO HAVE EYES THAT CHANGE
COLOR DEPENDING ON THE
MOOD THAT YOU'RE IN
- OR -
TO HAVE HAIR THAT
CHANGES COLOR BASED ON
THE TEMPERATURE?

WOULD YOU RATHER...

WEAR UNCLEAN CLOTHES FOR
A WEEK
- OR -
WEAR THE SAME OUTFIT
EVERY DAY FOR A WEEK?

GO TO SUMMER CAMP
- OR -
GO TO SUMMER SCHOOL?

WOULD YOU RATHER...

STROKE A FRIENDLY LION
THAT'S AWAKE
- OR -
AN UNFRIENDLY LION WHILE
IT'S ASLEEP?

SWIM OUTDOORS
- OR -
SWIM INDOORS?

WOULD YOU RATHER...

CLEAN UP YOUR BATHROOM
- *OR* -
CLEAN UP YOUR BEDROOM?

WIN A CASH PRIZE
- *OR* -
WIN A MYSTERY ITEM?

WOULD YOU RATHER...

BE ABLE TO SPIT OUT FIRE
- OR -
BE ABLE TO SPIT OUT ICE?

JUST WATCH A FOOD FIGHT
- OR -
BE IN A FOOD FIGHT?

WOULD YOU RATHER...

GET LOTS OF CUDDLES
- OR -
GET LOTS OF HUGS?

GO CAMPING
- OR -
GO FISHING?

WOULD YOU RATHER...

WAKE UP EARLY
- OR -
GO TO BED EARLY?

HAVE A DOLPHIN FOR A BEST FRIEND
- OR -
BECOME A DOLPHIN YOURSELF?

WOULD YOU RATHER...

HAVE A WATER BALLOON
FIGHT
- OR -
A SNOWBALL FIGHT?

HAVE A CAR THAT CAN
DRIVE UNDERWATER
- OR -
HAVE A FLYING CARPET?

WOULD YOU RATHER...

HAVE 3 CATS
- *OR* -
1 DOG?

DRIVE IN A CAR
- *OR* -
FLY IN A PLANE?

WOULD YOU RATHER...

BE ABLE TO RUN AS FAST AS A CHEETAH
- *OR* -
BE ABLE TO CLIMB WALLS LIKE A SPIDER?

HAVE FEET SO SMALL YOU HAVE TO SHOP FOR SHOES AT THE BABY'S DEPARTMENT
- *OR* -
HAVE REALLY LARGE FEET?

WOULD YOU RATHER...

LICK MILK LIKE A CAT
- *OR* -
YOURSELF LIKE A CAT?

HAVE YOUR FRIEND FORGET
YOUR BIRTHDAY
- *OR* -
FORGET YOUR FRIEND'S
BIRTHDAY?

WOULD YOU RATHER...

NEVER BE ABLE TO LISTEN
TO MUSIC AGAIN
- OR -
TO ONLY BE ABLE TO LISTEN
TO MUSIC FROM THE 60'S?

HAVE YELLOW EYES
- OR -
HAVE GREEN EYES?

WOULD YOU RATHER...

GO TO CLASS IN YOUR
UNDERWEAR
- OR -
WEAR PAJAMAS TO CLASS?

NEVER HAVE TO HAVE A
SHOWER EVER AGAIN
- OR -
NEVER HAVE TO BRUSH YOUR
TEETH EVER AGAIN?

WOULD YOU RATHER...

STICK WITH YOUR OLD
FRIENDS AT A PARTY
- OR -
MAKE NEW FRIENDS AT A
PARTY?

GET PRESENTS YOU DON'T
LIKE ON YOUR BIRTHDAY
- OR -
GET NO PRESENTS AT ALL?

WOULD YOU RATHER...

READ A HARDCOVER BOOK
- OR -
LISTEN TO AN AUDIOBOOK?

HAVE REALLY WHITE SKIN
- OR -
HAVE BLUE SKIN LIKE AN
ALIEN?

WOULD YOU RATHER...

BE THE WORLD'S RICHEST
PERSON
- **OR** -
HAVE THREE FREE WISHES?

SHARE YOUR BED WITH
SOMEONE WHO TALKS IN
THEIR SLEEP
- **OR** -
SHARE YOUR BED WITH
SOMEONE WHO SNORES?

WOULD YOU RATHER...

GO TO A CLOTHING STORE
- OR -
TO A TOY STORE?

HAVE NO EYEBROWS
- OR -
HAVE PINK EYEBROWS?

WOULD YOU RATHER...

HAVE A NEWLY DISCOVERED
ANIMAL NAMED AFTER YOU
- OR -
HAVE A NEW CANDY NAMED
AFTER YOU?

BE TOO OCOLD AT NIGHT
- OR -
BE TOO HOT AT NIGHT?

WOULD YOU RATHER...

SNEAK INTO YOUR
NEIGHBOR'S HOUSE WHILE
THEY'RE ASLEEP
- OR -
SPY ON YOUR NEIGHBOR?

SCRATCH YOUR BUTT IN
PUBLIC
- OR -
SCRATCH YOUR ARMPIT IN
PUBLIC?

WOULD YOU RATHER...

MEET AN ALIEN
- OR -
MEET GOD?

HAVE POOP THAT SMELLS
LIKE STRAWBERRY
- OR -
BE ABLE TO POOP
CHOCOLATE?

WOULD YOU RATHER...

HAVE A LIBRARY IN YOUR
HOUSE
- OR -
GO TO THE LIBRARY?

BUILD A HAPPY SNOWMAN
- OR -
BUILD AN AWESOME SAND
CASTLE?

WOULD YOU RATHER...

HAVE AN ITCH THAT REFUSES TO GO AWAY
- OR -
HAVE AN ITCH YOU CAN'T SCRATCH?

JUST ONE SUPERPOWER FOR A MONTH
- OR -
HAVE A LOT OF SUPERPOWERS FOR ONE WEEK?

WOULD YOU RATHER...

HAVE THE ABILITY TO
BECOME INVISIBLE
- OR -
HAVE THE POWER TO READ
PEOPLE'S MINDS?

FALL ASLEEP IN CLASS
- OR -
FALL ASLEEP ON THE BUS?

WOULD YOU RATHER...

GO JOGGING
- OR -
GO RUNNING?

GET INTO TROUBLE WITH
YOUR PARENTS OVER
SOMETHING YOU DIDN'T DO
- OR -
SNITCH ON YOUR BEST
FRIEND ABOUT SOMETHING
THEY DID?

WOULD YOU RATHER...

HAVE TISSUE PAPER STUCK TO THE BOTTOM OF YOUR SHOE
- OR -
HAVE GUM STUCK TO THE BOTTOM OF YOUR SHOE?

BE POPULAR AMONG YOUR CLASSMATES
- OR -
BE POPULAR AMONG YOUR TEACHERS?

WOULD YOU RATHER...

RELAX BESIDE THE POOL
- OR -
GO SWIMMING?

FART IN AN ELEVATOR ON
YOUR WAY TO CLASS
- OR -
FART IN CLASS?

WOULD YOU RATHER...

BE STUCK IN A BOAT IN THE MIDDLE OF THE OCEAN
- OR -
BE STUCK ON A ROCKETSHIP FLOATING THROUGH SPACE?

HAVE A GIANT POOL
- OR -
HAVE A JACUZZI?

WOULD YOU RATHER...

BE GIVEN $10 EVERY
SINGLE DAY FOR THE REST
OF YOUR LIFE
- OR -
GIVEN $1,000 ONLY ONCE?

OWN 10 PUPPIES
- OR -
10 KITTENS?

WOULD YOU RATHER...

BE SURPRISED WITH A PONY
- *OR* -
FIND A PONY ON YOUR OWN?

EAT SOMETHING ROASTED
- *OR* -
EAT SOMETHING FRIED?

WOULD YOU RATHER...

CREEP INTO YOUR SIBLING'S ROOM AND SNUGGLE UP WITH THEM
- OR -
SLEEP ALONE WHEN IT'S RAINING HEAVILY?

HAVE A TUMMY THAT MAKES RUMBLING NOISES A LOT
- OR -
HAVE A REALLY FAT TUMMY?

WOULD YOU RATHER...

HAVE A REALLY LOUD VOICE
- OR -
HAVE A SQUEAKY VOICE?

HAVE ALL THE JUNK FOOD
YOU COULD EVER WANT
- OR -
HAVE ALL THE DRINKS YOU
COULD EVER WANT?

WOULD YOU RATHER...

LICK YOUR FOOT
- *OR* -
YOUR FRIEND'S FOOT?

MOVE TO A NEW HOUSE
- *OR* -
GO TO A NEW SCHOOL?

WOULD YOU RATHER...

NOT GET ANY FOOD TO EAT
FOR AN ENTIRE WEEKEND
- OR -
EAT FOOD OUT OF THE
TRASHCAN?

WORK AS A LION TAMER
- OR -
NOT WORK AT ALL AND HAVE
A PET MONKEY?

WOULD YOU RATHER...

MEET A FRIENDLY DINOSAUR
- OR -
MEET A FRIENDLY DRAGON?

HAVE BRIGHT GREEN HAIR
- OR -
BRIGHT PINK HAIR?

WOULD YOU RATHER...

BE THE RULER OF ANY
OTHER COUNTRY IN THE
WORLD
- OR -
BE THE PRESIDENT OF THE
UNITED STATES?

NOT BE ABLE TO TASTE
ANYTHING
- OR -
NOT BE ABLE TO SMELL
ANYTHING?

WOULD YOU RATHER...

BRUSH YOUR TEETH WITH KETCHUP
- OR -
WITH HOT SAUCE?

HAVE A SNAIL AS A PET
- OR -
EAT A SNAIL?

WOULD YOU RATHER...

HAVE LARGE HANDS
- OR -
HAVE LARGE FEET?

STAY YOUNG FOREVER
- OR -
GROW UP INTO AN ADULT
OVERNIGHT?

WOULD YOU RATHER...

EAT ON THE LIVING ROOM
COUCH
- OR -
EAT IN YOUR BED?

LIVE IN A REALLY NOISY
NEIGHBORHOOD
- OR -
IN A REALLY QUIET
NEIGHBORHOOD?

WOULD YOU RATHER...

GO FISHING
- OR -
GO HIKING?

KNOW HOW TO SPEAK SPANISH
FLUENTLY
- OR -
KNOW HOW TO SPEAK FRENCH
FLUENTLY?

WOULD YOU RATHER...

NEVER BE ABLE TO SMELL
AGAIN
- OR -
BE ABLE TO SMELL ONLY
BAD-SMELLING THINGS?

FORGET YOU HAVE FEARS
- OR -
FACE YOUR FEARS?

WOULD YOU RATHER...

KNOW HOW TO READ LIPS
- OR -
KNOW AND UNDERSTAND SIGN LANGUAGE?

HAVE HAIR THAT'S ALMOST TOUCHING THE FLOOR
- OR -
BE BALD?

WOULD YOU RATHER...

LIVE IN A BOAT ON THE
OPEN OCEAN
- OR -
IN A TREE HOUSE FOR THE
REST OF YOUR LIFE?

EAT YOUR FINGERNAILS
- OR -
YOUR TOENAILS?

WOULD YOU RATHER...

NEVER HAVE PIZZA, EVER
AGAIN
- *OR* -
EAT A YEAR'S WORTH OF
PIZZA IN A SINGE NIGHT?

BE ON A TINY BOAT
- *OR* -
ON A GIANT SHIP?

WOULD YOU RATHER...

GO SEE A REAL LIFE SHIP
- OR -
GET A TOY BOAT?

HAVE A PET DINOSAUR
- OR -
HAVE A PET DRAGON?

WOULD YOU RATHER...

BE SURROUNDED BY
ANNOYING PEOPLE
- OR -
HAVE NO FRIENDS?

TO READ REALLY SLOWLY,
BUT UNDERSTAND WHAT YOU
READ REALLY FAST
- OR -
BE ABLE TO READ REALLY
FAST, BUT NOT UNDERSTAND
IT?

WOULD YOU RATHER...

LOOK REALLY OLD
- OR -
LIKE A NEWBORN BABY
AGAIN?

BE IN A DISNEY MOVIE
- OR -
BE IN A DISNEY ANIMATION?

WOULD YOU RATHER...

FLY IN THE SKY WITH THE
BIRDS
- OR -
SWIM IN THE OPEN OCEAN
WITH THE DOLPHINS?

PET A GIRAFFE
- OR -
PET A HIPPOPOTAMUS?

CPSIA information can be obtained
at www.ICGtesting.com
Printed in the USA
LVHW081946271121
704611LV00027B/926